SCHIRMER'S LIBRARY
OF MUSICAL CLASSICS

Vol. 1565

BACH

Six Suites
For Violoncello Solo

Revised and Edited

by

FRITS GAILLARD

G. SCHIRMER, *Inc.*

DISTRIBUTED BY

HAL•LEONARD®
CORPORATION
7777 W. BLUEMOUND RD. P.O. BOX 13819 MILWAUKEE, WI 53213

Printed in the U. S. A.

PREFACE

This revision of Johann Sebastian Bach's "Six Suites for Violoncello Solo" has been undertaken only after years of playing and studying them. As a part of the work of composing this revision, I have compared the readings of the original MS.[1] with those in the various editions, even the very first ones,[2] which are in my library. All changes suggested herein are inspired by a constant desire to preserve the spirit rather than the exact letter of the original. In the body of this edition, all departures from the original MS. appear between parentheses. Following this Preface, moreover, are several further suggested revisions, the adoption of which is left to the choice of the player.

Most important to an understanding of these works is an appreciation of the contrast between their lyric and rhythmic elements.[3] I have tried to indicate clearly the differentiation between them, which the player should constantly keep in mind.

The exact nature of the dance forms of the period should likewise be understood. Bach did not write any marks of expression in his suites, assuming that everyone understood the nature and tempi of the dances, which were a part of the idiom of the day.

The preludes do not fall into the same category as the dance movements. They are not built on a definite pattern; therefore they require close individual study. Each has its own particular character.

A word should be said about the *scordatura* in Suite V. In this instance, it involves the lowering of the A-string to G. Every note appearing above that G should be played on this lowered A-string. The depression of the first string not only improves the tone-color but also makes possible the playing of chord passages which otherwise would have to be altered to suit the regular Violoncello tuning. For the best results in playing this suite, it is advisable to use an A-string that is not too light.

It should also be mentioned that the extreme technical difficulty of Suite VI arises from the fact that it was originally written for a five-stringed instrument, now obsolete, known as the Viola Pomposa, invented by Bach himself. A simplified version of the latter portion of the Prelude has been included in the ensuing list of optional revisions offered to the player for his consideration.

FRITS GAILLARD

[1] By "original MS." is herein meant the Anna Magdalena Bach MS. in the Staatsbibliothek, Berlin.

[2] The two oldest and very first editions of the suites in my library are those of H. A. Probst (Leipzig: 1825) and Fr. Kistner (Leipzig: n. d.).

[3] Frequently, throughout this edition, dashes appear above notes. These dashes are not meant as tenuto-strokes, and notes thus marked should not be held beyond their proper value. Instead, these dashes indicate a melodic accent.

Suggested Versions

Suite II, Prelude, last 5 measures:

Original

These chords should be executed as arpeggios. Emending the E in the second chord to an F, I should suggest as an alternative version to the one appearing on p. 9*:

Suite II, Menuet I, 2nd measure:

Suggested version

Suite III, Bouree I, last measure:

Suggested version

Suite III, Bouree II, last measure:

Suggested version

Suite IV, Allemande, 7th and 8th measures after repeat:

Suggested version   Suggested version

Suite V, Prelude, 49th measure after the change to $\frac{3}{8}$ meter:

Original   Suggested version

Suite VI, Prelude, 22 measures from end:

Simplified version

Suite VI, Prelude, 11 measures from end:

Simplified version

Suite VI, Sarabande, 6th measure:

Original   Suggested version

*The version on p. 9 is by Grützmacher.

Six Suites for Violoncello Solo

Revised by Frits Gaillard

Johann Sebastian Bach
(Composed about 1720)

Suite I

Prelude*

* The headings of the movements are given as they appear in the original MS., except where otherwise noted.

4

Allemande

Courante

Menuet II

Menuet I D.C.

Gigue

8

Suite II

Prelude

Allemande

Courante

Sarabande

Menuet I

Menuet II

Menuet I D.C.

Gigue

Suite III

Prelude

Allemande

Courante

Sarabande

Bouree I

Bouree II

1st time I p

2nd time II pp

Bouree I D.C.

Gigue

Suite IV

Preludium

Allemande

Courante

Sarabande

Bouree I

Bouree II

Bouree I D.C.

Gigue

Suite V

Prelude

38

Allemande*

*In the original MS. this movement is incorrectly headed Courante.

Courante

40

Sarabande

Gavotte I

Gavotte II

Gavotte I D.C.

Gigue

Suite VI

Prelude

Allemande

Courante

Sarabande

Gavotte I

Gavotte II

Gavotte I D. C.

Gigue